BEGINNING WITH MARY

WOMEN OF THE GOSPELS IN PORTRAIT

Thomas John Carlisle

GRAND RAPIDS

WILLIAM B. EERDMANS PUBLISHING COMPANY

*This book is dedicated with
love and appreciation
to my wife,
Dorothy Mae Carlisle*

Copyright © 1986 by William B. Eerdmans Publishing Co.
255 Jefferson Ave. S.E., Grand Rapids, Mich. 49503
All rights reserved
Printed in the United States of America

Reprinted, February 1988

Library of Congress Cataloging-in-Publication Data

Carlisle, Thomas John.
Beginning with Mary.

1. Women in the Bible.   2. Bible. N.T. Gospels —
Biography.   I. Title.
BS2445.C37 1986 225.9′22′088042 [B]   86-11570

ISBN 0-8028-0914-3

PREFACE

The women of the Gospels are different — different from anyone you have ever met, different from women in any other time of human history. And yet there are many ways in which they are like us. We can learn from them as friends. We can appreciate them as extraordinary people.

Do not expect the women in this book to be like the Old Testament women I wrote about in *Eve and After*. This book is not a sequel to *Eve and After* but a companion volume.

Do expect this book to be different but even more pertinent to our lives. Here you will find not suspenseful stories but poignant portraits recreated from a minimum of information. Here you will find a quieter kind of heroism, the kind we need so desperately in our world today.

Using a line from one of my poems about Emily Dickinson, I called the Old Testament women "demure as dynamite." These Gospel women are "demure as dynamite" too, but in a very different way, one that makes more demands of our imagination and our personal creative approach. As much as possible, we need to discover how to see these women as Jesus saw them — as important persons in their own right. He treats them not as objects to illustrate the marvel of his ministry but as real people, needy people, caring people, responsive people, faithful people, heroic people.

You may wonder why this book does not include women from the remainder of the New Testament. Certainly they are important too. We wish we were told about more of them as well as told more about them. Perhaps they will be subjects for another group of poems. But they are not part of this collection because they did not have the opportunity to share in Jesus' earthly ministry.

As the title of this book suggests, it does begin with Mary, the mother of Jesus. It also includes some other important Marys as well as a number of other women who were devoted to Jesus and proved themselves invaluable to his ministry. Mother Mary comes to us in Section One. These other dynamic women are presented in Section Five.

You will find women whom Jesus helped/healed in Section Two. According to biblical record, each of these women had a single, special experience with Jesus. But it is entirely possible that some of them saw him at other times (Peter's mother-in-law probably did) and even became his followers. That may be a reason for their being remembered and included in the Gospels.

It disturbs me to observe that none of these ten women is even called by name. If you count them, you will discover that of the seven episodes recorded, three of them include two women: Peter's wife and her mother, Jairus's daughter and his wife, and the Syrophoenician woman and her daughter. How easy it is to see only one woman in each instance, but Jesus would have us see them both.

Sections Three and Four are the briefest. The "women on the fringes" in Section Three may not seem important. But they are a part of the Jesus story, and that makes all the difference. The women in Section Four are used by Jesus for illustrative purposes, but we are to perceive them as vivid nonetheless. Unfortunately, some of them have been badly neglected in Gospel preaching and the pertinence of others has been omitted or misunderstood.

Many people found the study guide at the end of *Eve and After* very useful, both for individual and for group study. Since such a guide is not included in this book, you may want to refer to the one in *Eve and After* for helpful suggestions about how to read poetry most fruitfully as well as for the kind of questions to raise in getting acquainted with women of the Bible.

As with *Eve and After,* I will offer cassettes of my reading of the poems in this book. You can obtain them by writing to me at my home, 437 Lachenauer Drive, Watertown, N.Y. 13601.

In the course of preparing this book, my enthusiasm for these Gospel women increased to the point where I feel I might even recognize them if a meeting were possible. My admiration has intensified to the degree that I am convinced that they are among the choicest people who have ever lived. Come and see whether you agree with me.

APPRECIATION

All those whose insights and encouragements contributed to the successful completion and publication of *Eve and After* have had an impact — sometimes indirect, often direct — upon this new book. Again I express my gratitude to all of them.

Beginning with Mary presented many more problems than *Eve and After*. It was much more difficult to compose illuminating poems. Perhaps this was the result of conditioning. We tend to be more familiar with the women of the Gospels to the point that we think of them as one-dimensional characters, appendages to Jesus' ministry but not people about whom to get excited or with whom we can identify. Some of my earlier poems on this theme failed to get past that barrier. Therefore, I am particularly indebted to those who were kind — and courageous — enough to challenge the adequacy and appeal of some of those poems. The question became, Must I give up my project, or can I become more creative and discover illuminating insights which poetry would intensify?

A great number of people were gracious enough to read all or parts of my developing manuscript with a friendly but critical eye. Without their cooperation, these poems might never have become a book. My wife, Dorothy Mae Carlisle, has given me most in the way of stimulus and specific questions and recommendations. I am also indebted to our sons — Rev. Jonathan T. Carlisle, Rev. David L. H. Carlisle, the Rev. Dr. Christopher Davis Carlisle, and Thomas Dwight Carlisle — and to my sister, Elizabeth Carlisle Lewis.

Others whose perusal of the poems has been of value and consequence include Rev. John B. Smiley, James Dowd, Prof. Joan Donovan, Wilfreda Stone, Judy Mathe Foley, Ellen Roberts Young, Marian Sengel, the Rev. Dr. William Randolph Sengel, Carolyn Payne, Patricia Forman, Linda Roberts, Janice Fry, Constance Metzger, Hazel K. Phipps, Rev. Russell Champlin, Ethelwyn George, Sheila Fairbairn, Sr. Anne Hogan, and Msgr. William B. Argy.

In addition, I am indebted to many of the readers of *Eve and*

After who both demanded and encouraged this second book.

My editor, Mary Hietbrink, has guided *Beginning with Mary* with exceptional expertise and understanding.

While there are many prose writings paralleling my theme, those which have been most useful and inspirational to me are *Jesus According to a Woman* and *Jesus and the Freed Woman* by Rachel Conrad Wahlberg, the third chapter of *Women and Ministry in the New Testament* by Elisabeth M. Tetlow, and *The Women Around Jesus* by Elisabeth Moltmann-Wendel.

My basic inspiration, of course, comes from the Gospels themselves, as I have read them again and again and anew and anew.

THOMAS JOHN CARLISLE

ACKNOWLEDGMENTS _____

The author wishes to thank the following publications, in whose pages certain of these poems first appeared, for permission to include them in this book:

alive now!: "I Have Called You Friends," "Generous Investors"
Christian Century: "The Annunciation," reprinted from the December 12, 1984 issue, copyright © by the Christian Century Foundation; "Footnote to History,"* reprinted from the April 10, 1968 issue, copyright © by the Christian Century Foundation.
Christian Living: "Revised Version," "Demotion," "Always More"
Church Management — The Clergy Journal: "Mary Magdalene," "Mary, the Mother of James and Joses," "'Many Others,'" "More Than One"
Episcopalian: "Always More"
Gospel Herald: "Puzzle and Provoke," "Witnesses of the Resurrection"
Presbyterian Life: "Shelter Me Now,"* "Assignment"
Presbyterian Survey: "Joanna"
Purpose: "Testimony," "Night Watch," "Talk Back"
Together: "Memory Bank," "Under the Influence," "Gratified"**

The following poems first appeared in *Mistaken Identity,* a book of poems the author published in 1973: "Well-Spring," "Aroma," "Common Knowledge" (entitled "Science"), "Justification," "Representative."

*These two poems subsequently appeared in *Celebration!* by Thomas John Carlisle (1970).
**These three poems subsequently appeared in *Mistaken Identity.*

CONTENTS ⸺⸺⸺⸺⸺⸺⸺⸺

FOREWORD _____

Why is it that writing poetry about women of the Gospels is so very different from writing poetry about women of the Old Testament — and so much more difficult? This has been my experience, but it is not a simple matter to understand why. I would like to share with you some of my dilemmas and observations.

The women of the Old Testament had to make it completely on their own in a patriarchal culture which discouraged their independence and initiative. They also suffered the disadvantage of being of the same sex as the female goddesses worshiped by their pagan neighbors. These goddesses were associated with the fertility rites which the prophets were quick to denounce as immoral and contradictory to ethical monotheism.

Thus, most of the women whom the masculine authors of the Hebrew Bible include in the narrative are strong, liberated, fascinating people whose stories could not have been omitted without strong protest. Nevertheless, these stories tend to be minimized or given less attention than they would have received if their protagonists had been men. Take Miriam as an example. In a poem I wrote about her in *Eve and After,* I described her as a "supportive sister," "emanicipation's mouthpiece," a "skillful administrator in triumvirate," "Moses' challenger," as a "blend of tenderness / and toughness this Miriam / poet and prophet." Yet all this highly significant information had to be gleaned from a few verses in Exodus and Numbers.

Or consider the Wise Woman of Tekoa, whose story is told in II Samuel 14. She is an extremely skilled and sympathetic peacemaker, but the chronicler gives Joab most of the credit, as though he could have accomplished this worthy purpose with a less able co-conspirator. Abigail in I Samuel 25 is another peacemaker. Abishag is invaluable to David, but only five verses in I Kings 1 tells us about their relationship.

Among numerous others who are scarcely mentioned and even less frequently given attention or credit are the courageous and witty midwives in Exodus 1, Pharaoh's daughter in Exodus 2, and the Woman of Thebes in Judges 9, who successfully prevented a war.

Once we learn about these stories and pay them proper attention, we realize how exciting they are. So are such longer and well-known dramas as those of Sarah, Deborah, Ruth and Naomi, and Vashti and Esther.

When we come to the New Testament, however, the situation changes. True, the culture remained patriarchal, and women were still treated as second-class citizens from both religious and civil standpoints (which for the Jews were one and the same). But the women of the Gospels found, to their surprise, that they had a friend in Jesus. He characteristically and consistently treated them as full persons rather than as the weaker and inferior sex. And they responded enthusiastically to his encouragement and his esteem. Nevertheless, at first we may not think these Gospel women are nearly as dynamic as the women of the Original Testament. What explains this? First and foremost, the fact that Jesus is the hero of almost every episode in the Gospels, including those episodes in which women appear.

Because of their tremendous admiration for Jesus and their masculine bias, the Gospel writers not only accentuate (rightly) the strength of Jesus, but seem to go out of their way to stress the negative or weak tendencies of some of the women — ill health, for example. Yet it is significant that they cannot help but include many episodes in which women appear in a favorable light. We may be able to ascribe this to the fact that women held a place equal to that of men in the very early church.

Through the centuries, male clergy in their sermons have been inclined to ignore most of the Old Testament women, and have not given equal time or respect to the women of the Gospels. It is unfortunate that the traditional lection-aries fail to include such magnificent stories as that of the paralyzed woman in Luke 13:10-17. Of course, Jesus *is* the hero of the Gospels. But we are denying Jesus' own attitude if we think of the women simply as foils or adjuncts to his teaching and his acts of healing.

It is natural for us to look at Jesus, but it is essential that we look at the persons Jesus looked at — people to whom he gave his liberating and re-creating power. It is amazing that the Gospels do highlight so many women, but this is the case because Jesus did so. Jesus thought they were important, and he treated them accordingly. They responded with faith and an understanding and comprehension which is less ob-vious and less frequent in the responses of men.

Much is made of the fact that "the Twelve" were all men. This accords neatly with the number of the tribes of Israel. Yet the three great leaders of the church were Peter, James (the brother of Jesus), and Paul, and only Peter was one of the Twelve. Thus it was not long before the early church ceased to treat this correlation as being of any primary importance. It is also interesting to note that the Gospels give us some information about Peter, John, James, and Judas, but supply very few details about several of the others, and give nothing but the names of the rest. In addi-tion, it is difficult to reconcile the lists of disciples in the various Gospels to determine precisely who they were, or if there were in fact exactly twelve.

Even more important is Jesus' definition of discipleship. Upon examining the Gospels, we discover that the women are more inclined to act like disciples than are the men. Many of the women accompanied Jesus along with the men (who numbered more than twelve) on their "missionary" journeys. But we have been led to assume that their service was limited to some narrow definition of "women's work" — fixing meals and washing and mending clothes.

However, on careful reading we discover that some of the named and unnamed women financed the expeditions, though no man is credited with doing so. Yet we seem to dismiss their contribution as not particularly important, despite the fact that in those times business matters were not considered the province of women. If we rethink the matter, their financial backing may remind us of the rare action of Queen Isabella of Spain, who underwrote Christopher Columbus's voyage to the New World. Indeed, the Gospel women outmatched her: Queen Isabella did not accompany Columbus, whereas the Gospel women traveled with Jesus and took full part in his expeditions.

Now and again we are specifically told of a woman's proclaiming the Gospel, but it is likely that such proclamation occurred much more often than the records indicate. Have we stopped to consider that Martha's declaration of faith in Jesus as the Christ (John 11:27) is at least equal to Peter's (Matt. 16:16)?

The women of the Gospels were apt pupils and followers who applied what Jesus taught. These are two main marks of discipleship. The men of the Gospels did not serve very well in this latter regard, especially when it came to the Cross. "They all forsook him and fled" (Mark 14:50). And although John, at least, went to Golgotha, it was the women who stayed faithfully "beneath the cross of Jesus." It was also women who were first at the tomb on Easter morning and became the bearers of the good tidings. Apparently Mary Magdalene was the first person to encounter the Risen Christ; Matthew indicates that another woman — Mary, the mother of James and Joses — was with her.

None of this makes women better than men. But all of this does point to the fact that women were notable among the full-fledged followers of Jesus, disciples in consonance with Jesus' definition of that word. It is time that we recognized and rejoiced in this inclusive situation.

This requires us to be more sensitive to the personalities about whom the Gospels give us some inkling. When we read their stories afresh, we discover that "passive" is not the word for these women. A number of them talked back to Jesus and may have contributed to the development of his thinking. At least one showed a sense of humor, a delightful specialty of Jesus that seems to be utterly lacking in Gospel men. The retorts of these women were strong yet consistently constructive, not tricky and insincere like the remonstrances and caviling of the Pharisees. (It is interesting to note that the Pharisees were all males.)

Recognizing the exciting contributions and participation of these women may force us to discard many preconceived notions. It should inspire us to read the Gospels more perceptively and with greater devotion to discovering more about Jesus himself.

If we find ourselves at first inclined to respond to the stories of these women as uninteresting or unimportant, let us ask ourselves why. True, these accounts are not filled with the suspense or the militance which we find in the accounts of Old Testament women. And it is also true that we are provided with even less information about notable Gospel women than we are given about Old Testament women. But we need to focus on the fact that greatness has been defined by Jesus himself in far different terms than those of a Cecil B. DeMille movie or a dynastic soap opera or a television miniseries. Are we willing to accept the challenge to recognize that goodness and service are beautiful and indispensable even though they do not have us sitting on the edge of our chairs?

The story of Jesus is thrilling once we become receptive to the wonder and glory of it. We will not be able to do this fully until we treat as important everything that he treated as important. Because we may have been insensitive in the past to the importance with which he treated people — women, children, men — we miss the impact of the greatest story ever told, the greatest life ever lived.

So now I am beseeching you to read the Gospels again, not only receptively but as though you had never read them before. I am asking you to pay special attention to the attention which Jesus gave to people because this is what we have tended to neglect most. I ask you to note particularly the high dignity and sensitive understanding which he accorded to women in a time when a woman's word was inadmissible in a court of law, when a woman was forbidden to study the scriptures.

Near the beginning of *Eve and After* is "Look at Me," a poem in which a biblical woman speaks to us:

Come, look at me again and try to dream
the woman I was in that far long ago.
My hair style and my dress may set me off

as ancient, but I beg of you to know
the actual person I was — the thoughts which I
carried in my heart — no photograph could show
or artist's sketch — the essentials of my self —
the woman alive in this portfolio.

I believe that Jesus wants us to see in this three-dimensional
way what these women of the Gospels meant to themselves,
what they meant to Jesus, and what they can mean to us.

THOMAS JOHN CARLISLE

1 Mary, Mother of Jesus _____

THE ANNUNCIATION
(Center Panel from the Mérode Altarpiece
by Flemish Artist Robert Campin,
Circa 1425 - 28) _____

An ordinary room with everyday
furniture, utensils, common floors and ceiling.
Mary is there. We see no open door.
As yet unseen by her, an angel kneeling
preludes the proclamation God has given.
The window blinds are partly open, where
billows of clouds are figured. From another
oval of aperture the Spirit's seven
gifts penetrate to fill the future mother,
and we perceive the marriage of earth and heaven.

Luke 1:26-38

ELIZABETH

THE VISITATION _____

She shared her feelings with Elizabeth
who recognized her coming as a sign
they two had been impressed into a role
concordant with the grace of the divine
purpose and plan. Excitement filled their talk
as though each babe was calling to the other.
High dreams of Israel's hope burst into song:
the joy, the mission granted to a mother.
Children to be prepared for great events
that those who bore them might not comprehend.
How much it meant to share the faith, the fear,
the anticipation with a trusted friend.

Luke 1:39-56

2

MAGNIFICAT _____

If Mary had sung
her song of songs
with our accustomed
unmagnificence
and dearth of urgency,
all the commitment
all the charm
and all the challenge
and anticipation
would have been
completely dissipated.

O sing anew
anew
anew
the simple song
which magnifies
rejoices
dares to vision
the fall of kings,
the exaltation
of the small
unviolent
trusting and faith-full
servants
of the spectacularly
creative God.

Luke 1:46-55

RHAPSODY IN RED _____

O Mary
lyricist of liberation
singer of freedom's song
and orchestrator
of the emancipation
proclamation which your son
would herald to the world,

what inspiration
clothed your words
with such fire and spirit
dictators dread
the impact
of your revolutionary
rhapsody?

Luke 1:46-55

REVOLUTIONARY CAROL _____

Like Hannah, Mary
knew how to sing
the topsyturvy upsidedownside
good news carol
for the poor and hungry,
victimized, oppressed.

At our eternal peril
we choose to ignore
the thunder and the tenor
of her song,
its revolutionary beat.

Luke 1:46-55
1 Samuel 2:1-10

4

SHELTER ME NOW _____

Shelter me now
from the cold
she said
Shelter me now
while I bleed
and bear the child
whose coming is joy

Shelter me now
from the sheep
and the strangers
who sleep
in our stable

Shelter me now
(and she smiled)
Lift him now
There is room
in the manger

Luke 2

5

A BLESSÉD EMBARRASSMENT _____

Mary is a blesséd embarrassment
to a harassed world

for she is great in more ways than one
and we wonder how she managed

to contain the salvific secret
seeing all that she had seen and heard.

How absurd, say all the knowing,
unknown as we are to such magnificence.

What guidance, what star, what manger
can cradle our indifference?

An offense against our apathy
this pathetic refugee mother.

But what other birth will ever be able
to make us strong and stable with shalom —

home again in the world God made.
Home with Mary's — and Joseph's — aid.

WONDER WOMAN

Mary the wonder woman
in whose womb
the galaxies are knit
and God emerges
as a peasant child
whose word and wounds
doom all the powers of darkness.

ONLY MARY

It is only Mary, just Mary,
the insignificant, the unknown
who is known of God.
Her low estate rocks kingdoms
then and now.

ANNA

EXPECTANCY

Anna and Simeon waited all their lives —
not to behold a perfect no-hit game,
not to survey the skies for some new comet,
not to collect a lottery or sweepstakes —
but for the coming of Christ into the world.

How low our level of expectancy!

WITHOUT THE GOSPELS

Paul's single recorded
allusion to Mary
is the one word
woman.
"Born of a woman,"
so he summed it up.

Which seems to show
that, valuable
as his epistles are,
we would be poor indeed
without the Gospels
and their humane portrayal
of the Christ Paul preached,
who took his first
uncertain steps
as Mary's little boy.

Galatians 4:4

I AM YOUR MOTHER

I am your mother and I have a right
to be upset about your disappearance.
How could we guess that you weren't with the neighbors
or with our relatives if not with us?
The Nazareth caravan was big enough
to keep you safe without our close surveillance.
How could you do this stupid, thoughtless thing
and leave me limp with frenzied desperation,
a trauma I will carry to my grave?

The city isn't safe for one young boy.
The Temple itself hides its own depths of dangers.
A sword has pierced my heart, as Simeon said.
Yes, I am shaken — and relieved — and angry.
I have no oath or pledge as Hannah had
when she left Samuel to serve old Eli
and traveled home without him. You did wrong
to scare me so — and I forgive you for it —
but never again go traipsing off like this
without informing me of your intention.
I don't want anything to happen to you —
not now or ever. Are you listening?

Luke 2:35, 41-50
I Samuel 1:11

IN THE TEMPLE

How did his mother —
and his father — feel,
forgetting to ascertain
his presence
and failing then
to find him
till at last
in the least likely place
in the haphazard
sequence of their searching
they came across him
doing business
in his God Father's House?

INITIATOR

Who instigated the action at the Cana wedding?
Who saw and felt the embarrassment of her friends,
the domestic crisis, the near disaster,
liable to extinguish the festivity?

This Jewish mother chose to prompt her son,
to quell and quench his quiet remonstrances,
to take command in the emergency,
save face and save the day which meant so much.

"Do what *he* tells you — anything he tells you,"
she ordered the servants. They obeyed her word
and his. They took the six stone water jars
and filled them to the brim, and their new contents
brought sparkle to the guests and glad relief
to those who were credited with saving best for last.

John 2

REVISED VERSION _____

His family thought
he was out of his mind
and needed them
to come take charge of him.

Not so very
different from
our attitude
toward Jesus.

He must have been
out of his ever-loving mind
to say what he said
and do what he did.

So we revise
his words,
touch up
his portrait.

We take charge.

Matthew 12:46-50
Mark 3:31-35
Luke 8:19-21

11

ASSIGNMENT _____

Is there anything
I can do
for you?
I politely
inquire
of my distressed
friends
fancying
the answer
is No.

Standing
by the cross
of Jesus
I conjecture
there is nothing
that can be
done
for his comfort
at this late
date
no last
request
He might address
to me.

Instead
He says
Behold
my mother
my sister
my brother
all yours.
Take care
of them
for me.

John 19:26-27
(related to Mark 3:32)

MARY THE DISCIPLE

It may have been
more meaningful for Mary
to be her son's disciple
than to be his mother.

FOOTNOTE TO HISTORY

Did she choose to raise
the question of invasion
of her privacy and her grief
when they all demanded
to know everything
she could remember about him
after his murder?

Their mental tape recorders
meticulously memorized
various curious commentary,
her early anguish warning,
jokes he told during supper,
flowers he brought home from field trips,
quips about the Establishment,
and odd words of the poor and wise
who first stopped by to see him.

Most of it they chose to leave
out of their final versions.
She was not authorized
to insist on additions
or criticize or alter
what they called gospel truth.
Never even saw a copy
source though this Mary was.

2 Ten Women Jesus Helped / Healed _____

THE WAY IT HAPPENED

Were Mark and Matthew
Luke and John aware
how many women
were the subjects
of Jesus' incidents
of grace and healing?

Telling it like it was
serves to illuminate
the equal opportunities
accorded to all.

How providential!

DEMOTION

We have defeated Jesus —
temporarily —
by relegating
to inferior status
people he sought
to treat as equals.

What a shame!

LIFTUP _____

Jesus was always
lifting people up
literally
and figuratively,
physically
and spiritually
but it all began —
the Gospels tell us —
when the mother
of Peter's wife
needed a house call
and he came
and stilled the fever,
turned her malady
to melody,
her infirmity
to vigor.

Mark 1:29-31

PARTNER IN LOVE _____

Healed by his care,
she cared enough
to voluntcer
her services:
partner in love
of Jesus'
ministering mission.

Mark 1:29-31

ALL RELATIONSHIPS _____

He raised a mother's son.
He healed a father's daughter.
The configurations
of his compassion
are unlimited.
He is the generous genius
of all relationships.

Luke 7:11-17,
Mark 5:21-24, 35-43

A NEW BEGINNING _____

She was a widow,
I her only son.
My death was her
destruction.

But Jesus saw
her overwhelming need
and said, "Don't cry" —
so I am told —
and brought about
a happy ending
to the story
and a new beginning
for me.

Luke 7:11-17

I AM JAIRUS _____

I am Jairus
and I get impatient
when I am interrupted
or frustrated
in even my smallest
plans and projects.

But Jesus baffles me
not only by his power
but by his patience.

I was overjoyed
when he agreed
to come to visit
my dying daughter
with his healing touch
and presence.

But on the way
he stopped to help
a hemorrhaging woman
and the delay
seemed like a lifetime. . . .
And so it was —
for friends arrived to say
my daughter had died
and Jesus need not come.

But Jesus came.
He doesn't give up —
not easily.
He strode right through
the weeping and confusion
to her room.

I couldn't believe my eyes
nor could my wife
when Jesus called my daughter
and took her by the hand
and raised her from the bed
and she began to walk
around the room.

We were excited
and never stopped to think
what she might need
at this particular moment.
But Jesus bade us give her
a bowl of broth,
a bit of fish.

It seems to me
that Jesus thinks of everything.
But should I be surprised?

Mark 5:21-24, 35-43

THE MOTHER _____

I am the mother
of the little girl
whom Jesus raised
from death. I cannot guess
how he could manage
such an unheard-of thing.

I saw it for myself.
I heard his words —
"Daughter, arise" —
and watched my child
obey him.

I never thought
to get her food
but Jesus noticed
and so I brought her bread
and honey and milk.

My husband had the faith
to go to Jesus
while I stayed by her bedside
till he came.
And we are all
the richer for his presence.

Mark 5:21-24, 35-43

TALITHA CUMI _____

My father tells me
he was driven crazy
by the apparent procrastination
of Jesus after he had promised
to visit our house and save me
from certain death.

My father's urgency
was driven to desperation
when Jesus stopped
to speak with a contaminated
woman who had placed
her trembling fingers
on a tassel of his robe.

It seemed an eternity
to my fretful father
before Jesus was ready
to travel on.
But then the word arrived
it was too late.

Just as Jesus ignored
the pleas of those who pressed him
to ignore the invalid woman,
so he ignored
the counsel of the friends
who said it was no use
to bother the teacher further.

But Jesus kept on coming.
On arrival
he walked right in
to where I was,
past all the crying and commotion.
He took me by the hand
and said, "Talitha cumi" —
"Dear little girl, get up."

I know all this
being told so many times.
And I certainly remember
walking around the room
and seeing my mother and father
and hearing Jesus say
"Give her some food."

It was worth waiting —
no matter how long —
for Jesus to appear.
I think I know now
why some people call him
in deed the resurrection and the life.

Mark 5:21-24, 35-43

THE WAY TO LIFE _____

We know he knew
the way to life.
He did and does.

Mark 5:35-43

22

DAUGHTER _____

Jesus repudiated
the ugly and unjust taboo
which avowed
a woman's blood
made her and others
unclean.

Jesus accepted —
and welcomed —
the audacity
of one who touched
in faith
his garment's fringe.

Not satisfied
not to encounter
her face to face,
he turned and asked,
"Who touched me?"

Her acknowledgment
exhilarated him.
He gave her peace
in the place of fear
and a more generous
and thorough healing
than she had dared to hope.

And — best of all —
he called her *Daughter*.

Mark 5:25-34

23

DESPISED AND REJECTED _____

She was despised
and rejected of men
because she was
a woman —
with an illness
peculiar to women.

No physician
had ameliorated
her harrowing
and humiliating
condition.
Many had made her worse.

She touched him
and the power
of his wholeness
and the compass
of his compassion
united to give her
health and peace.

Her engagement
with Jesus
meant new life for her
and all her sisters
stigmatized
by society's
insensitive legalities.

Mark 5:25-34

EMANCIPATION PROCLAMATION ___

Jesus had no desire
to wash his hands
of her.

He chose
to treat her
not as unclean

but as a daughter
of Israel
in full and equal
standing.

His emancipation
proclamation
was not confined
to her alone.

It was a new deal
for every woman.

Mark 5:25-34

IN THIS STORY ___

Saved by the blood
has another
and novel
application.

Mark 5:25-34

25

HEADLINES _____

The woman gets the headlines
in the scandalous story
which Jesus turned around —
and so should we.

The adulterous men
deserve the notoriety
which Jesus gave them
when he circled the sand
and they slunk off
to ponder — or ignore —
the sins which left them
pointing the finger of shame —
and blame —
straight at themselves.

John 7:53-8:11

LASTLY _____

Jesus was not good
at throwing rocks
at sinners —
a trait
which made his enemies
gang up on him,
sometimes with stones
and lastly
with a cross.

26

ACCUSATIVE CASE _____

They made the woman stand
as object lesson
and tried to trap the teacher
as one who violated
old laws and customs.
They accused her
in order that
they might accuse him.

He put the finger
on their specious case
and hammered against
their hearts of stone
and sent them packing
once they calculated
who the wicked were.

John 7:53-8:11

WAITING _____

The woman waits
for Jesus' word.

Might I?

John 7:53-8:11

NATURE AND NEED _____

Humility was not
my nature
or my need.
I had to argue back
to save my daughter —
at least to try
to save my daughter.

I heard him say
he came to save
his chosen people,
not Gentile dogs —
which seemed to leave us out.
And so we had no claim
on either his power
or his kindness.

Nonetheless, I became
much more fractious
and presumptuous.
What had I to lose?
I cared so much
that he should heal my child
I told him even the puppies
under the master's table
could salvage crumbs.

I think he laughed out loud
at my rebuttal.
He appeared to appreciate
what he appraised
as cleverness and wit
as well as faith
and urgent love.

He said that he would do
what in my desperation
I had begged.

And I went home
and found my daughter well.

Matthew 15:21-28
Mark 7:24-30

THE SYROPHOENICIAN WOMAN
AND HER DAUGHTER

RECIPROCATION _____

A twinkle in his eye,
the contours of kindness,
belied insensitivity
his words implied.

I tried again.
I answered him in kind
and he reciprocated
with healing for my daughter
and for me.

Matthew 15:21-28
Mark 7:24-30

DAUGHTER OF THE
SYROPHOENICIAN WOMAN_____

At last I learned
the risk my mother took
in challenging
the foreigner
whose word had power
to heal the mind
and heart.

I like to think
that I inherited
her spark and spunk,
her skill in disputation,
her shrewd sharp agile wit
to speak the winning word.

I was the one
to prompt the raconteur
to set the story straight.

I ought to know!

Matthew 15:21-28
Mark 7:24-30

JESUS RAISED ME _____

I could not straighten up.
It is not easy
to see the world
from such a crooked angle
and keep one's sanity
and smile when others
laugh at the warp
of my infirmity.

They should thank God
for the most precious gift
of being able to stand erect
but it never occurs to them
except when they observe
someone like me.

They are so sure
it could not happen to them
so they are not inclined
to try to feel my pain
and my frustration.

I would be crippled still
but Jesus raised me
to my full height —
in many more ways than one.

Luke 13:10-17

31

WHAT JESUS DID AND DIDN'T DO _____

The things which Jesus did *not* do
are most illuminating.
He did not wait.
He did not hesitate.
He did not list
the reasons why
he should do nothing.
He did not look askance
or look away.
He did not ask
for a morality clearance
on her character.
He did not ask her
what the doctors said
or didn't say
or did or didn't do.
He saw her as a human being,
as a sister,
a friend,
a daughter of Abraham,
a child of God.
Although she long had been
a prey and victim
of paralysis,
crooked and crippled
and dispirited,
he nonetheless
visioned her
as the woman
she was meant
to be.

He saw *her,*
set her straight
by word and touch,
and she gave God
the glory and gratitude
for her fantastic freedom.

Luke 13:10-17

THE BENT-OVER WOMAN

LOOSED

They saw no problem
on the Sabbath day
in loosing ox or ass —
untying it from the manger
and leading it to water —
or in rescuing
an animal
which had tumbled
into an open well,
but they were hurt
and horrified
to see a woman
bent double
be loosed
from her infirmity,
set free
from the bondage
of her body's pain
and for the outreach
of her soul.

Luke 13:10-17

RESURRECTION _____

He called me woman
in the same honorable way
he would address his mother.
The name
took on a radiant meaning
as I rose
from my constricted past,
my years bent over
with crush and crunch
of my unliftable
burdens and desperations.

When he named me daughter —
daughter of Abraham —
I felt the glory
and I knew
that nothing could ever
hold me down again.

Luke 13:10-17

THANKS GIVING _____

Sometimes my gratitude
is instantaneous
like that of the bent woman
Jesus freed.

More often
a delayed reaction
or a fuse
refusing to go off.

34

3 Women on the Fringes_____

IN LINE WITH JESUS _____

Jesus' ancestors
include some prominent people
like Abraham,
Isaac and Jacob,
and, of course,
King David
plus a plethora
of less distinguished men.

Less noticeable perhaps
but pertinent
in their impertinence
and relevant
to scripture's stress
and emphasis
we find four women
who made a shocking
and resounding splash
in history
as well as genealogy:

Tamar, who bore
the twins of incest
but proved more righteous
than her famous
father-in-law;
Rahab, the innkeeper
or scarlet woman
of Jericho
who saved the spies
and subsequently
successfully defected
and became
a Mother in Israel;

Ruth, an unlanded immigrant
and frightened foreigner
who spent the night
at Boaz' feet
before he recognized her
as his wife;
and beautiful *Bathsheba,*
here identified at first
as brave Uriah's wife
who in due time
became the bride
of David.

A fascinating foursome
singled out
as memorable
appropriate
and worthy ancestors
to one who,
in a world
managed by men,
gave women
a glad and equal
recognition.

Matthew 1:3, 5, 6

THE WIVES OF THE DISCIPLES _____

The wives of the disciples did not make
the list of those who, leaving for Christ's sake,
would be rewarded many many fold
once they had died or grown too weak and old
to draw the dividends reserved for them.
Some may have stayed in Cana, Bethlehem,
Capernaum, Kerioth — wherever they
had chanced to live upon that sudden day
when heaven took their husbands by the heart
and set them to a business far apart
from fishing, tax-collecting, or whatever
their role had been. It hardly took a clever
woman to know when "No" would never do.
Their men said "Yes" and they would see it through
perhaps even as far as a cross might take them.
This Nazareth man had some strange power to wake them
from minor loyalties to old routines.
He filled their racing minds with splendid scenes
of the one kingdom worth life's pearl to find.
So what becomes of those they left behind?
Were some among the mothers — why not wives? —
who went along to share their ardent lives,
help with the meals, the laundry, and the preaching,
and listen to the zenith of Christ's teaching?
Even the ones who had to stay behind
with children — or from choice — were sure to find
their spouses coming home to share a while
the force and flavor of their Lord's life-style.
The little land where people walked so far
could bring them not "as punctual as a star"
but often enough, and closer when they came
than in the days before Christ lit the flame
of "Follow me." Then wedded to work they were,
now more to him, so naturally to her,
each felt, since love was what his cause was all about.
We hope each wife was quick to find this out.

DOOMED? _____

I am Salome.
Must I be
the image of my mother?
Her commitment
to lust
and murder
is her ablest talent.
I detest
her perverse joy
in watching me dance
and watching her husband leering
while trusting his lechery
to achieve the prize
of John the Baptist's
head upon a platter
in my obedience
to her whim
and her polluted purpose.
I dance
but wonder why.
Am I, Salome,
doomed and destined
to be another
Herodias
and not a new
woman in my own
fair right?

Matthew 14:1-12
Mark 6:14-29

HIS SEEING _____

Was it my sin —
or even my husband's —
that our baby
was born in darkness?
How his little face
would turn to try
to place my voice.
And as he grew
his heart and mind
struggled to create
my countenance
in vain.

In vain until the day
that Jesus took
matters into his own hands —
spat upon the ground
and packed the clay
on our son's eyes,
commanding him to go
to Siloam's pool to wash.
Miraculously
the treatment worked
like magic
like a charm
and our son came seeing
with a song of joy.

I do not know
why we are questioned
doubted
vilified
for simply telling
God's own truth.

Why is his seeing
such a dangerous thing?

John 9

40

JESUS KNEW

She had given
her last
and little coins.
She had no more
to give
but Jesus knew
how great the gift,
how true
his own strange words:
Blessed —
yes, blessed —
happy
are the poor.

Mark 12:41-44
Luke 21:1-4

SHE KNEW THE JOY _____

Money was welcome
from anyone —
even from those
who were not men.

That is why
they graced the Temple
with a treasury box
in a convenient place
inside the Court of Women.

So she stole
surreptitiously
to give her little
to the God she loved.

Her money outmatched
the most the mightiest
paraded for the public's
praise and approbation.

Her heart was full.

Mark 12:41-44
Luke 21:1-4

DREAMS DENIED _____

How did Pilate's wife
know about Jesus?
From rumors alone?
Or word from her maidservants?
Or some chance meeting
with this memorable man?

She said that she had suffered
much because of him —
all in a dream.
But was it a dream only?
Was her conscience hurt
because she lacked the courage
of Joanna
to leave her palace post
and follow the Crown Prince
of truth
and liberation?

She was convinced
that he was innocent
of public crimes
but not unguilty
of stirring her heart to dreams
she had denied.

Matthew 27:19

TESTIMONY _____

She dared
to speak a word
for Jesus
when it counted.

Matthew 27:19

BACKSTAIRS AT THE HIGH PRIEST'S HOUSE _____

My tasks are menial
my wages small
and no security
social or otherwise
goes with this job.
My chores require
my attendance
all over this palace
which the high priest
makes his home.

His politics
mean nothing to me.
I am aware
his business
is intricate
and intriguing
quite beyond
my caring
or my understanding.
Still, at times
I overhear
the desperate
or pregnant sentence
which makes me wonder
what is going on.
Why is he now upset
because a Galilean teacher
is trying to hawk
the wares of God?
What competition
can that be to him
since his religion
is so fundamental
and so impregnably
established?

The Temple
is his kingdom
or it was
until the first day
of this present week.
The Galilean came
and slammed things 'round,
and said the place was God's
and not a market.
Now I would never think
of going there to pray.
The Gentile's Court
is always far too noisy.
The Women's Court
strikes me as second-rate,
inferior,
which is what we are —
or how we are treated.

There is a bustle
in the house tonight
something to do
with this man Jesus.
I guess I'll go
fetch fuel for the fire
out in the courtyard
where some men are huddling.
God, it is cold!
Perhaps among them
are some hangers-on
who think that Jesus
is a king or something
and do not dare
to show their faces
while he faces
the Sanhedrin.

I think
I hear
a Galilean voice.

Mark 14:66-70

WITNESS? _____

Ready to accuse
but not to sympathize
with the beleaguered man
who falters and denies.

Matthew 26:69-70
Mark 14:66-70
Luke 22:56-57
John 18:16-17

LIKE THE DAUGHTERS
OF JERUSALEM _____

We are readier
to weep for others
than to face the facts
of what our listlessness
and luxury
allow in damming up
the streams of righteousness
and lovingkindness.

If we knew
the noose we tighten
on our nation
with our faith
in guns and greed,
we would be weeping
for ourselves
for our intransigence
and our stupidity
and then would dry our tears
and shoulder to shoulder
push the Sisyphus stone
until we bury it
in the New Jerusalem.

Luke 23:28

46

4 Women of Jesus' Parables and Other Teachings _____

ALWAYS MORE

Jesus' stories
never come out even
with pat and perfect answers.
There is always one to carry
or two or three or four!

The infinite possibilities,
the open-ended
requirements
and insights
leave us breathless
as we discover
how incalculably far
ahead of us
he always is.

PUZZLE AND PROVOKE

Jesus enjoyed
his inconsistencies
since each involved
a generous helping
of the ambiguous
truth. He knew
that parables
make better
and less lucid
guides than proverbs.
And his words
still puzzle
and provoke us
and provide us clues
which trouble
and redeem.

HOW LIKE A WOMAN _____

How like a woman
    to do the same old household chores
    (getting the meals and sweeping the floors)

How like a woman
    to lose the precious thing she most should keep
    (like a careless shepherd losing one prize sheep).

How like a woman
    to find the coin and then to call her friends
    to share the joy of how the story ends —
    the best of being human.

And how like God.

Luke 15:8-10

NIGHT WATCH _____

We mock the foolish virgins
who neglect to keep their eye
on their supply of oil
but fail ourselves
to bring the requisite lamp
or even journey
to the wedding feast.

Matthew 25:1-13

49

AS WERE THE FIVE _____

We exclude ourselves
by taking lightly
Jesus' injunction
to keep our oil flasks full
and to be all and always ready
as were the five
whose lamps lit the night
as soon as the shout rang out
"The bridegroom comes."

Matthew 25:1-13

CHALLENGER OF THE UNRIGHTEOUS JUDGE

VINDICATION _____

Why did Jesus tell
this story?
What was he trying
to prove?
Or did they try
to find a proper moral —
one more pious
than this obscure vignette
seemed to portray?

Since Jesus said it,
why not be satisfied
with what it clearly
indicates:
his pleasure
at justice
for the poor
and powerless
triumphing
because of her
aggressive fidelity
to her cause.

Luke 18:2-5

50

ILLUSTRATION _____

A strong
and self-respecting woman
would not knuckle under
to an unjust judge
or any predator
of her consumer
or other human
rights. Jesus applauded
this iron-willed widow
for her persistence
and tenacity
in seeing the case through
and gaining the justice
due to her
in an unscrupulous
and cruel world.

He lifts her up
as a most beautiful
and cogent illustration
of perseverance
requisite for prayer
to God the righteous
and compassionate Judge.

Luke 18:1-8

FINALLY _____

Because she
would not give up
he finally
gave in.
Justice was served
despite his long disservice.

Luke 18:2-5

AT TOO LONG LAST _____

It served him right
that she kept after him
because he had not
done right by her.

Like a small boy
who knows that he
has disobeyed
his mother,
at too long last
he did what had been right
from the beginning
but proceeded to give
his own wrong reason
for his overdue decision.

But justice was served.

Luke 18:2-5

THE FEMINIZATION OF POVERTY _____

Poverty has always been
the special province
of women — the widow
or abandoned wife
valueless without a husband.
Protected by laws
meagerly or rarely
enforced — or by no laws
at all. Object
of the compassion
of uncompassionate people.
Subject to her devotion
to the fatherless child
or nest of children.
Prey to prejudice
as to market value
or untrained and welcome
in the menial
and misprized occupations.

What pedestals
they are allowed
to stand on
and starve.

SOMEBODY'S WIFE _____

Whose wife would she be
in the resurrection
(if there should be one)?
Seven husbands
might claim her
as their property.
What a grim dilemma!

No one thought of asking
whose husband a man would be
if he outlived
a plethora of spouses —
as men often did.
That did not fit their plot.

Women were not supposed
to be so durable.
Frequency of pregnancy
and the vicissitudes of childbirth
took a lethal toll.
Perhaps sterility could be a blessing
and barrenness have some benefits.

She who had seven times failed
to bear a child
was not to be left out
in Jesus' estimate.

Heaven does not perpetuate
the inequities of earth.
Though treated as a no one here
God provides for her and others
a revised and reasonable
appraisal.

Worth trying now.

Matthew 22:23-32
Mark 12:18-27
Luke 20:27-40

ENLIGHTENMENT _____

At first I was indignant.
It sounded so undignified
to have Jesus
called Child.
Baby at Christmas
did not faze me —
or Boy inquiring
in the Temple
at twelve.
But Child —
instead of Son —
of God
seemed demeaning,
and I winced
and wished
that they would leave
the Bible alone —
although the Bible
is left too much alone
even by me.

And then
in one enlightening flash
it came to me:
Jesus insisted
that the best way
to enter the realm of God
is to become
like a child.
So now I know
it isn't a bad word
after all
but brings new light
regarding One
who is
Light of the World
and light and life
to me.

APT METAPHORS _____

The women in his audience
were glad
that he acknowledged them
in what he said.
From childhood
he had observed, appreciated
the things they knew —
the power of leaven,
for example,
and the way that birth
made one forget
the waiting and the labor
in jubilation
that new life has come.

Matthew 13:33
Luke 13:20-21
John 16:20-22
(See also John 3:3)

THE FOREMOST FUNCTION _____

Mary was more —
as every woman is —
than female physiology.

Jesus did not deny
the blessedness of motherhood
but did reject
the naming of a woman
by the parts
not given to men
while overlooking
the foremost function
of us all —
to know and do God's will.

Luke 11:27

JOURNEY? _____

The Queen of the South
came all the way from Sheba
that she might meet
notoriously wise
and celebrated Solomon
and hear his words.

What journey would we take —
of body or mind —
to hear the message,
grasp the greatness,
recognize the sovereignty
of Jesus?

Matthew 12:42
Luke 11:31

5 The Eleven Other Women Disciples (Besides Mary) _____

THE REAL DISCIPLES _____

Who were the real disciples?

Those who served,
who cared how Jesus felt,
who understood the other side of failure,
who followed to the cross,
who shared its pain,
who traveled to the tomb
with tears and spices
and met the miracle of Easter morning.

They were the real disciples.

THE WOMEN DISCIPLES _____

The women disciples
are not dramatic
and exciting
like the men.
None betrayed him,
none denied him,
none insisted
on misunderstanding
in the accounts we treasure.
They did not hesitate
to argue or to offer
their own opinions
but they were always ready
to recognize the tenor
of his teachings
and take him seriously
at full face value
and follow with tenacity
and devotion
no matter what
the cost.

RELUCTANT CHRONICLERS _____

They were not eager
to keep telling
of the conspicuous part
the women played
through all the Gospel story.

But they could not help it
since Jesus helped these women
so notoriously,
so openly,
and since they helped him
joyfully
and sacrificially.

The writers chose to tell
only the parts
they had no choice
but to include,
so known and noted
were these episodes.

And so we know
of Mary Magdalene,
of Mary and Martha,
of Salome,
and a surprising company
of others who
accompanied
or encountered
him.

EXCEPT HERODIAS ⸻

How ironic
that in the Gospels
it is always men
who are betraying
or denying
or disbelieving
or failing
to understand
and women never
get blamed for anything!

OUTDOOR MINISTRY ⸻

It may have been that Jesus
chose the ministry
of town and countryside
(thus not confining himself
to synagogue and Temple)
so that the women
who desired
to follow him —
to be disciples
and proclaimers
of his witnessed word —
could share his crucial
and creative company.

OMISSION

In pondering
the women disciples
of Jesus Christ
I find the Gospels
fail to tell me
of any who
betrayed him
or denied him.

I don't know why
I'm not surprised.

THEIR CALL

They didn't have to be
called. They came.
His invitation
was unspoken
but authentic.
Their response
was genuine
far-reaching
all-embracing.
Their commitment
complete
and unconditional.

THREADING THEIR WAY _____

One of the threads
that runs through all
the fabric of the Gospels
is the faith
the faithfulness
the understanding
the women demonstrated
while many of the men
were constant
in their propensity
for getting twisted
into knots
and then unraveling
when most he needed
them.

THE WOMEN _____

They followed.
They listened.
They learned.
They served.
They spoke
both with and for him.
Thus they qualified
as bona fide disciples.

THE WOMAN OF SAMARIA _____

Her blemishes, major and picayune, had prompted
her travel alone at noontime to the well,
yet this Samaritan whom Jesus met
has much — so very much — to tell.

A whole theology unfolds as we
are listening to that crucial conversation.
She is a woman — yet he talks with her —
Samaritan, and Jews despise her nation.

She is no scholar though she has the talent
to raise the probing questions and to claim
there can be worship any place where people
aspire and care enough to call upon God's name.

She learns the metaphor of living water
with which old Jacob's well cannot compare.
She reaches out with faith in the Messiah
and learns that Christ himself is sitting there

talking with her, sharing eternal truth.
She hastens home without her water jar
to tell her neighbors her discovery —
personal, universal, singular.

She brings a large and eager throng to Jesus,
she whom they had despised and criticized.
Her words and her experiences lead them
to hear, believe, receive the living Christ.

John 4

WELL-SPRING _____

Was he well favored?
Well, we do not know.
Well fixed he was not
but we say well born.
Well spoken — to put it mildly.
Well disposed.
Well grounded
in the things that matter most
and able to tell
the depths of import
at a random well.

John 4

MISSING THE MESSAGE _____

We miss the message
Jesus emphasizes —
his revelation
of his plan and purpose
and person.

Why does he choose
a woman at the well
to tell the new, new story
of his Christhood?

Why is she
the first to preach
the Gospel of his coming?

Why are women
entrusted and instructed
to go and tell
when he is risen?

Why are we
so dense to the import
of his words and deeds?

John 4

TALK BACK _____

Talking back
to Jesus
is as lucrative
as talking back
to God.

It yields
new answers
and new insights.

And it takes spirit —
the right spirit,
bold and open
to new truth.

John 4

MARY MAGDALENE _____

My "sin" was sickness.
My afflicted mind
was captured by devils.
They filled my days with fear
and nights with frenzy.
I was impotent
to cure —
or to forgive —
myself.
And then he came.
Perhaps he called me Mary.
So many times since
he has called me Mary
I can't remember.
But I do remember this.
He called me and recalled me
to myself
and made me whole and healthy
and so marked
with joy and gratitude
I cannot do
enough for him.
And so I follow
anywhere he goes
and I will not deny him.

Matthew 27:55-61; 28:1-10
Mark 15:40-47; 16:1-11
Luke 8:1-2; 24:1-11
John 19:25; 20:1-2, 11-18

CHARACTER-ISTIC ERROR _____

She has been mistaken
for someone else
this Mary —
Mary of Magdala.

There is no evidence
to prove her prostitute
or even spectacular sinner.

Her mind was ill —
perhaps her body too —
and Jesus healed her.

And she shared
her wholeness with the world
superlatively.

MEMORY BANK _____

Her memory bank
was full
of ghosts
and devils
till he withdrew
the gross.

He paid
her debts
with prodigal
munificence.
She knew
how much.

UNDER THE INFLUENCE _____

Under the influence
of Jesus
she caught
the melody
of sensibility
a faith feeling
for another's
needs.

She ran
the raw risk
of rejection
the misery
of maybe
misunderstanding
or being
misunderstood
the Judas-word
of waste
or raucous
ridicule.

Once touched
she touched.

HIGH ADVENTURE _____

She left her husband
to go on
toadying to Herod
while she
breathed the clean air
.of high adventure
and an uncommon cause.

While Nicodemus
only dared to visit
Jesus by night, Joanna
came by day —
and every day.

What headlines her
radical activities provoked
in their edition
of *National Enquirer.*

It would be like her
to listen at Gethsemane.
She climbed to Calvary.
She verified
the Arimathean tomb.
She tasted
the awe and ecstasy
of Easter morning.

JOANNA

Joanna —
emancipated
by his healing touch —
risked all
left all
gave all
for Jesus,
a genuine
disciple
if there ever was one.

AT JEOPARDY

A traitor to the state,
some certainly called her,
a heretic
to Herod's High Society,
she committed herself
to go the way of Jesus.

What jeopardy!
What joy!
What rare fulfillment
became the portion
of this genuine
Joanna.

Luke 8:3; 24:10

THEY RAN THE RISK _____

They were not
Jesus' "groupies"
though they ran
the risk of such
a reputation.

Their engrossment
had other chaster,
purer, more profound
dimensions.

Their devotion
and their dedication
issued from what he did
not only for their lives
but for the lives of others.

His charismatic words
daily pierced their ears
and satisfied their hearts.

Friendship and worship
mingled in their stance
toward him.

And their fidelity
encouraged and sustained
his cause.

Their countenances
confessed, confirmed,
communicated
his power
to bring new Eden
to the world.

SUSANNA _____

I am Susanna.
There is little else
the Gospel records tell
about me,
though I am given
credit for resourcefulness.

I shared
in Jesus' travels
and his mission
and helped maintain
his tenuous treasury.

It is enough
to be one of the many
healed by his word,
companion to his cause
and ready to tell
how much he did
and daily does
for me.

Luke 8:1-3

SUSANNA TO JESUS

Jesus, I do not fully understand
just what you mean
by least and greatest.
From the beginning
I was willing and eager
to be of service
in every way I could.
It was never my goal
or purpose to be great
but rather to capitalize
on the great
opportunity
to be with you
to hear your words
and act upon them.

You taught me how
to be my own best self,
conscious of the potential,
of the talents I have.
You taught me
there is nothing wrong
with being a servant —
even a slave —
when this involves
loyalty to the high
and holy purpose
you have revealed
to me and many others
not only by the miracle
of your living words
but by the total way
you incarnate them.

You are the servant
and I choose to be
as much like you
as life allows me.

I would be least
in that best sense
you show me.

Luke 8:3; 9:48c

GENEROUS INVESTORS _____

One of the mysteries
of Jesus' ministry
is where the money
came from. There is no
evidence of taking
an offering or making
an appeal for funds,
no honoraria
for his unscheduled
speaking engagements.

Among the generous
who subsidized his cause
were women who invested
the resources they had.
Apparently they poured
their money like precious
ointment to enable
Jesus to travel
up and down the land
with all he had to offer.

THE GIFT OF GRATITUDE _____

Nothing
is too good
for Jesus.
That's the way
the man he healed —
Simon the leper —
appeared to feel
for he failed
to take any special care
to make Jesus comfortable
but simply let him be
one guest among a throng.
Nothing — only nothing —
was good enough
for Jesus.

But the woman
who washed his road-stained feet
(an apt example!)
with tears of gratitude
and precious perfume
and dried them
with her hair
with no concern
for what the "righteous" men
might say about her
was demonstrating
her opinion:
Nothing was too good
for Jesus
and doing everything
was still not good enough.

And she was right.

Luke 7:36-50

AROMA

Some see the courtesan
instead of the courtesy
the one she used to be
instead of the one she had become
thanks to his power
of reclamation
and beautification.
They try to discomfit her
for trying to comfort him
since they had no idea
of doing anything of the kind.
The stench of their dirty looks
is dissipated by the vial
of her abashed anointing.
His disappointment
in their pride and prejudice
yields to the redolence
of her response.

COMMON KNOWLEDGE

We know
the acutest methods
to detract
deflate
denounce
defame
trying to devalue
love's labors.

GRATIFIED _____

Amused
at the arrogant
who think
their need
for mercy
minimal

he smiles
to embrace
the tears and kisses
and scents
of this brave woman's
gift.

I HAVE CALLED YOU FRIENDS _____

Who were his friends?
The Gospels are so busy
describing male disciples
and their acts and questions
we wish we had a longer
list embracing those
whom he called friends
although they did not journey
with his constant
and committed
caravan.

We know a few
and so are certain
that he sanctified
the heart of friendship —
Joseph of Arimathea
and Nicodemus
seem to be,
but unmistakably
the trio at Bethany:
Martha
and Mary
and Lazarus.

THE BEST OF BOTH _____

Why was it
that Jesus chose
two women
to communicate
the *summum bonum?*

What Martha did
was good - -
no doubt about it.

What Mary did
may have been better —
though we tend to doubt it.

Sometimes one person
can incorporate
the best of both.

FEAST _____

Mary,
contrary
to men's
expectations,
your priority
was not to set
the supper table
or to fix
the food
though you were well
acquainted with both.

The best dish
of the evening
was to sit
and listen
and learn
and take a part
in the delicious
conversation.

You chose the better portion.

Luke 10:38-42

WHAT MARTHA SAID _____

Why didn't you come
when you were needed most?
We sent and said to hurry
but you lingered.
We are sure
if you had been here
Lazarus would have lived.
And even now I know
you have the power
if you should choose
to use it.

Now you are saying
if I hear aright
you are the resurrection
and you are the life
and that our faith in you
will conquer death for us.

Do I believe you?
Yes, I *do* believe
that what you say is true,
I do believe
you are the Christ we seek,
the very Son of God.

Come, see the place
where we have laid him.
Weep with us. . . .
And we will roll
the stone away
at your command.

John 11

A LAST SUPPER _____

Who were
the ministers —
the celebrants —
for that eucharistic meal
of food and word
at Bethany?

Martha and Mary
together prepared
the supper.

Martha served
the elements
and Mary
officiated
at the sacrament
of footwashing.

The house was filled
with fragrance
and significance.

John 12:1-8

REPRESENTATIVE _____

All those perfume accounts
present Mary as a better
abettor of his wares.
Perishable goods became durables
when handled with his concern.

John 12:3-8

ANOINTING _____

Anointing has a multiplicity
of meaning:
to cool, comfort, heal;
to celebrate with joy;
to prepare for burial;
or to acknowledge a king.

And Christ, The Anointed One,
embraces them all.

THE ANOINTED ONE
(Christos) _____

We call him Christ
over and over
and overlook
the meaning
of the name,
the impact
of the title,
and ignore
the wisdom
and the insight
of the women
who anointed him
to that high office
with no authority
but love.

DIFFERENT AND SIMILAR _____

The Gospels
love to tell us
the different stories
of the different women
who chose to spend
their expensive perfume
on the choicest person
they had ever met:
the characteristic
singular
and quintessential
expression of their love.

Matthew 26:6-13
Mark 14:3-9
Luke 7:36-50
John 11:2; 12:3-8

UNNAMED ANOINTER

LIKE AND UNLIKE _____

Like Peter and Judas
and John and James
I am enamored
of success —
unlike the unnamed woman
who dared to anoint
the king whose suffering
and death would bring
a topsy-turvy kind of kingdom
blest by God.

Mark 14:3-9

JUSTIFICATION _____

So strange
so sweet
so shocking
so absurd.
The rhyme and reason
of her reckless gift
have no excuse
but love.

IN REMEMBRANCE OF HER _____

Sometimes we remember
him. More often we forget
her diligence and love.

He does not say, "Do this."
She does it nonetheless.

She may have gone again
to anoint him in the dawn
when death and resurrection
faced each other finally.
That morning was too late.

But now she seizes
the aromatic instant.

Of the beauty of her deed,
within and beyond her means,
he said, "Remember."

Mark 14:3-9

IDENTITY AND DESTINY _____

Jesus' identity
and Jesus' destiny —
the servant king,
the suffering servant king —
attributed
attested to
celebrated
in his being anointed
at this woman's hands.

MARY, THE MOTHER OF JAMES AND JOSES _____

My sons are his disciples.
So am I.
Some think I follow them.
I follow Jesus.
He called me
without words
but with an appeal
which I had no desire
to refuse or question.
I try to do my part
in all the chores
our group requires
as well as tell
the story of the fullness
of God's glory
his life has given mine.
And I listen —
best of all, I listen —
and I love
and I will go
as far as following him
may some day take me.

Matthew 27:56, 61; 28:1-10
Mark 15:40, 47; 16:1
Luke 24:10
John 19:25

WHEN IT MATTERED MOST _____

No word that she said is recorded
but someone remembered she always
was there when it mattered most —
at the cross and
in the mysterious garden
where Jesus surprised them by saying,
"Good morning."

Matthew 28:9

WALKING THE GOSPEL ROADS _____

There are some
who manage to do more
than others,
paying no attention
to their own
strengths and virtues,
only concerned
to give and give and give
as the fulfillment
of their life and being.

Such was the militant
and warm and caring Mary
whom we identify
as mother of James and Joses.

She walks the Gospel roads
kind, gracious, and unflinching
and never stops to boast
how valuable she has been,
how valuable she is
to Jesus.

88

ALL THE WORLD _____

If this devoted Mary
is not only
mother of James and Joses
but the wife
of Clopas — or Cleopas —
the nuances
are multiplied.
And if we add
the possibility
she was related
to Mary and/or Joseph
we have a fascinating
interweaving
and relationship.
Was it her home
where Jesus broke the bread
and eyes were opened
when their guest
was visible no longer?

We do not know.
Perhaps we never will
but need we wish
for nothing to wonder about
or to surmise or speculate?

We can cherish
the all too partial portrait
we possess
of one who must
have meant so very much
to Jesus
just as he
meant all the world to her.

Luke 24:13-31
John 19:25

89

ALL BECAUSE _____

I am Salome,
wife of Zebedee,
mother of James and John,
those sons of thunder,
and a disciple of Jesus —
but not in that order.
The last comes first
though each
is precious in my sight.

Because of Jesus
I have had adventures
infinitely beyond
my most imaginative
childhood dreams.

Because of him
I've rearranged
all my priorities
and found the best
investment for my life.

Matthew 20:20-23; 27:56
Mark 15:40; 16:1-8

MORE CLOSELY _____

Salome gets overshadowed sometimes
by her extraordinary sons —
which was exactly
what she thought she wanted.

And yet she had a rich life of her own —
don't you forget it —
and she was willing
to travel places they might not
and listen — at times — more closely
to the words and meaning
Jesus had in mind.

SALOME'S STORY _____

Salome's story
is not limited
to her misunderstanding
of the kind of kingdom
her two sons
might find
pleasurable
and profitable.

She followed Jesus
even more faithfully
than most of the disciples —
even to Friday's cross
and Sunday's sunrise.

MOTHER OF MARK _____

Shall we count Mary
mother of John Mark
as one of his disciples?

We know her home
contained the upper room
where Christians met
to pray for prisoned Peter.

And was she hostess
to the farewell feast
the night he was betrayed?
That was an upper room
which someone whom he loved —
and trusted — offered him.
It could have been this woman
who shared the plot
and peril
and purpose
of that pascal evening.

She had an upper room
available for Jesus.

Acts 12:12

ROOM? _____ _____

There may have been room
in the upper room
for women
not primarily
for preparing food
or serving it
but definitely
for sharing at the table.

92

"MANY OTHERS" _____

"et cetera"
provides a most
convenient category
not only for things
but for people

we hear in passing
of the "other women,"
"many women,"
"many others,"
"many other women"

now and then
some names are given
but too often
they are not considered
worth naming

they are not
distinguished
but they are
illustrious
in Jesus' estimate
of greatness

Matthew 27:55
Mark 15:40-41
Luke 8:3; 24:10

EACH ONE WAS DIFFERENT _____

Each one was different
but all alike
in their allegiance,
in their desire
to understand the import
of his words,
in their determination
to contribute to his cause
with all the treasure
of their waking hours
and any money they had.
Nothing was menial
for he gave it meaning.
They accepted the cost
as needing no accounting.

We know too little
of all they did.
We know the names
of all too few.
But we rejoice
for all who followed him.

MORE THAN ONE

There was more
than one mother
at the cross.

There are always
more mothers
at the world's crosses
than we are able
to bear
to think about.

But if we did
perhaps there would not be
so many crosses.

AUTHENTICATORS

These women told
what they had seen
and felt
and shared
and so we know
the story of the cross
authentically.

Mark 15:40-41

IN THE EVENING SHADOWS _____

We scarcely see them
in the evening shadows
those women named Mary
sitting there in sight
of where the body of Jesus
is resting. They make sure
that he is safe at last
and they make certain
the way to journey
with their tears and spices
after the Sabbath is past.

We scarcely see them
in the evening shadows.

Matthew 27:61

LOVE COMES FIRST _____

They came to anoint
the body of Jesus
and could not
because it was too late
that early morning.

How glad they were
that others had anointed
(perhaps they too had done so)
while there was time
for him to enjoy
the pervasive fragrance
the refreshing fingers

the feeling of peace
this act provided.

How do we
go about
anointing Jesus?

Mark 16:1ff.
and other passages

WITNESSES OF THE RESURRECTION _____

Women are welcomed
as witnesses
of Jesus'
resurrection.
Their word
in a court of law
was valueless
but we rejoice
that one who loved
all people
came first
and now and again
to those
who knew
and loved
him well
and happened
to be
women.

WHO TOLD THE TWO? _____

Did you ever notice
who told the two
on the Emmaus Road
that Jesus' tomb
was empty?

Luke 24:22

SUSCEPTIVITY _____

When we try to picture
the women Jesus healed
and those courageous ones
who took their places
among his most
faithful and comprehending
disciples,
should we imagine them
as the average
church member
of our acquintance
or as the most
extraordinary
the most resonant
the most dynamic
and outreaching
in their response
to the great news of grace —
women made beautiful
by their susceptibility
to Jesus.

MORE THAN WE KNOW _____

Only in quiet excitement
can we find
the forever more
of one who walks
beside us
yet so far before.

ASCENSION _____

In the vicinity
of Bethany
he said *Goodbye*
for the last time —
or likely said
Shalom.
They did not comprehend
that they would never
see him again
or that always
his presence
would irradiate
their lives.

Luke 24:50

BEYOND THE BOUNDS _____

The stories point
beyond themselves.
They tell of women.
They tell
more than the tellers
realized they told.

And Jesus still
opens the scriptures
to new treasures for us
beyond the bounds
of our perimeters.